INSPIRATION

FOR

COOKS

INSPIRATION FOR COOKS

Summersdale Publishers Ltd
46 West Street
Chichester
West Sussex
PO19 1RP
UK

www.summersdale.com

Printed and bound in the Czech Republic

ISBN: 978-1-84953-633-2

Substantial discounts on bulk quantities of Summersdale books are available to corporations, professional associations and other organisations. For details contact Nicky Douglas by telephone: +44 (0) 1243 756902, fax: +44 (0) 1243 786300 or email: nicky@summersdale.com.

INSPIRATION

FOR

COOKS

EMILY DARCY

summersdale

There is no love sincerer
than the love of food.

GEORGE BERNARD SHAW

I cook with wine; sometimes
I even add it to the food.

W. C. FIELDS

Cookery is become an art,
a noble science.

ROBERT BURTON

I hate people who are not serious about meals. It is so shallow of them.

OSCAR WILDE

If more of us valued
food and cheer… above
hoarded gold, it would be
a merrier world.

J. R. R. TOLKIEN

After a full belly all
is poetry.

FRANK McCOURT

Oh, I adore to cook.
It makes me feel so mindless
in a worthwhile way.

TRUMAN CAPOTE

Life is a combination
of magic and pasta.

FEDERICO FELLINI

One cannot think well,
love well, sleep well, if one
has not dined well.

VIRGINIA WOOLF

Once you understand the
foundations of cooking —
whatever kind you like…
you really don't need a
cookbook anymore.

THOMAS KELLER

Cooking is like love.
It should be entered into
with abandon or not at all.

HARRIET VAN HORNE

An empty belly is
the best cook.

ESTONIAN PROVERB

A crust eaten in peace
is better than a banquet
partaken in anxiety.

AESOP

Tell me what you eat, and I
shall tell you what you are.

JEAN ANTHELME
BRILLAT-SAVARIN

Nothing is too much
trouble if it turns out
the way it should.

JULIA CHILD

My weaknesses have
always been food and men —
in that order.

DOLLY PARTON

Part of the secret of
success in life is to eat what
you like and let the food
fight it out inside.

MARK TWAIN

'Tis an ill cook that cannot
lick his own fingers.

WILLIAM SHAKESPEARE

You could probably get
through life without
knowing how to roast a
chicken, but the question is,
would you want to?

NIGELLA LAWSON

Nothing would be more tiresome than eating and drinking if God had not made them a pleasure as well as a necessity.

VOLTAIRE

All sorrows are less
with bread.

MIGUEL DE CERVANTES

Salt is born of the purest of parents: the sun and the sea.

PYTHAGORAS

Cooking is an observation-based process that you can't do if you're so completely focused on a recipe.

ALTON BROWN

Kissing don't last;
cookery do!

GEORGE MEREDITH

The more you eat, the less flavour; the less you eat, the more flavour.

Ask not what you can
do for your country.
Ask what's for lunch.

ORSON WELLES

Secrets, especially with cooking, are best shared so that the cuisine lives on.

BO SONGVISAVA

Life is unlivable to them
unless they have tea
and puddings.

GEORGE ORWELL
ON THE ENGLISH

I read recipes the same way I read science fiction. I… say to myself, 'Well, that's not going to happen.'

RITA RUDNER

Food is symbolic of love
when words are inadequate.

ALAN D. WOLFELT

Cooking is one of the oldest arts and one that has rendered us the most important service in civic life.

JEAN ANTHELME
BRILLAT-SAVARIN

He was a bold man that
first ate an oyster.

JONATHAN SWIFT

Tomatoes and oregano make it Italian; wine and tarragon make it French… garlic makes it good.

ALICE MAY BROCK

Preach not to others what
they should eat, but eat as
becomes you, and be silent.

EPICTETUS

Cakes have such a terrible
habit of turning out bad just
when you especially want
them to be good.

L. M. MONTGOMERY

Fish is the only food that is
considered spoiled once it
smells like what it is.

P. J. O'ROURKE

I like rice. Rice is great
if you're hungry and want
2,000 of something.

MITCH HEDBERG

We all eat and it would be
a sad waste of opportunity
to eat badly.

ANNA THOMAS

Cooking is at once child's
play and adult joy. And
cooking done with care is
an act of love.

CRAIG CLAIBORNE

The way you make
an omelette reveals
your character.

ANTHONY BOURDAIN

Always start out with a
larger pot than what you
think you need.

JULIA CHILD

My two rules of cooking:
keep it fresh and keep
it simple.

MIKE ISABELLA

Bring the same consideration
to the preparation of your
food as you devote to your
appearance. Let your dinner
be a poem, like your dress.

CHARLES MONSELET

All cooking is a matter of
time. In general, the more
time the better.

JOHN ERSKINE

But when the time comes
that man has had his dinner,
then the true man comes
to the surface.

MARK TWAIN

Don't eat anything
your great-great-great
grandmother wouldn't
recognise as food.

MICHAEL POLLAN

Be content to remember
that those who can make
omelettes properly can
do nothing else.

HILAIRE BELLOC

After a good dinner one can forgive anybody, even one's own relatives.

OSCAR WILDE

Everything you see,
I owe to spaghetti.

SOPHIA LOREN

Only the pure in heart can
make a good soup.

LUDWIG VAN BEETHOVEN

Cooking is not chemistry. It
is an art. It requires instinct
and taste rather than exact
measurements.

MARCEL BOULESTIN

Only a fool argues with a
skunk, a mule or a cook.

AMERICAN PROVERB

Forget love, I'd rather
fall in chocolate.

ANONYMOUS

Do not taste food while you're cooking. You may lose your nerve to serve it.

PHYLLIS DILLER

A man may be a pessimistic determinist before lunch and an optimistic believer in the will's freedom after it.

ALDOUS HUXLEY

It is the sauce that
distinguishes a good chef,
and the saucier is a soloist
in the orchestra of a
great kitchen.

FERNAND POINT

The ambition of every cook
must be to make something
very good with the fewest
possible ingredients.

URBAIN DUBOIS

Good bread with fresh
butter, the greatest of feasts.

JAMES BEARD

Most seafoods should be
simply threatened with heat
and then celebrated with joy.

JEFF SMITH

The kitchen is a country
in which there are always
discoveries to be made.

GRIMOD DE LA REYNIÈRE

Gourmandise is an impassioned, rational and habitual preference for all objects that flatter the sense of taste.

JEAN ANTHELME
BRILLAT-SAVARIN

If a pot is cooking, the
friendship will stay warm.

ARABIC PROVERB

Fish, to taste right, must
swim three times — in water,
in butter and in wine.

POLISH PROVERB

A recipe has no soul.
You, as the cook, must bring
soul to the recipe.

THOMAS KELLER

Listen carefully to me, and eat what is good, and delight yourselves in abundance.

ISAIAH 55:2

Food is life, life is food.

KEITH FLOYD

The only real stumbling block is fear of failure. In cooking you've got to have a what-the-hell attitude.

JULIA CHILD

I like a cook who smiles
out loud when he tastes
his own work.

Robert Farrar Capon

When you have the best and
tastiest ingredients, you can
cook very simply and the
food will be extraordinary.

ALICE WATERS

Cooking requires confident guesswork and improvisation – experimentation and substitution, dealing with failure and uncertainty in a creative way.

PAUL THEROUX

Cooking is all about homes
and gardens; it doesn't
happen in restaurants.

DELIA SMITH

The greatest dishes are
very simple.

AUGUSTE ESCOFFIER

Banish the onion from the kitchen and the pleasure flies with it.

ELIZABETH ROBINS PENNELL

Don't cook steaks in the
toaster, even little ones.

P. J. O'ROURKE

A recipe is only a theme,
which an intelligent cook
can play each time.

Madame Benoît

Eat all the junk food
you want as long as you
cook it yourself.

MICHAEL POLLAN

Cooking demands attention,
patience, and above all,
a respect for the gifts
of the earth.

JUDITH JONES

Wo was his cook but if
his sauce were Poynaunt
and sharp.

GEOFFREY CHAUCER

Ingredients are not sacred.
The art of cuisine is sacred.

TANITH TYRR

A well-made sauce will
make even an elephant or a
grandfather palatable.

GRIMOD DE LA REYNIÈRE

I don't like gourmet cooking
or 'this' cooking or 'that'
cooking. I like good cooking.

JAMES BEARD

Garlick maketh a man
wynke, drynke and stynke.

THOMAS NASH

If you have a constant,
unwavering desire to be a
cook, then you'll be a
great cook.

THOMAS KELLER

A cake is a very good test
of an oven.

DELIA SMITH

A good cook is a peculiar
gift of the gods. From the
brain to the palate, from the
palate to the finger's end.

WALTER SAVAGE LANDOR

This is every cook's opinion –
No savoury dish without
an onion,
But lest your kissing should
be spoiled,
Your onions must be
fully boiled.

JONATHAN SWIFT

Carve a ham as if you were shaving the face of a friend.

HENRI CHARPENTIER

So long as you have food
in your mouth, you have
solved all questions for
the time being.

Franz Kafka

When a man's stomach is
full it makes no difference
whether he is rich or poor.

EURIPIDES

If God had intended us to
follow recipes, he wouldn't
have given us grandmothers.

LINDA HENLEY-SMITH

Recipes don't work unless
you use your heart.

DYLAN JONES